This book is dedicated to Mrs. Johnson.

Books on Strike
Copyright © 2023 Jennifer Jones
All copyright laws and rights reserved.
Published in the U.S.A.
For more information, email info@ninjalifehacks.tv
ISBN: 978-1-63731-730-3

Find the Books on Strike lesson plans at ninjalifehacks.tv

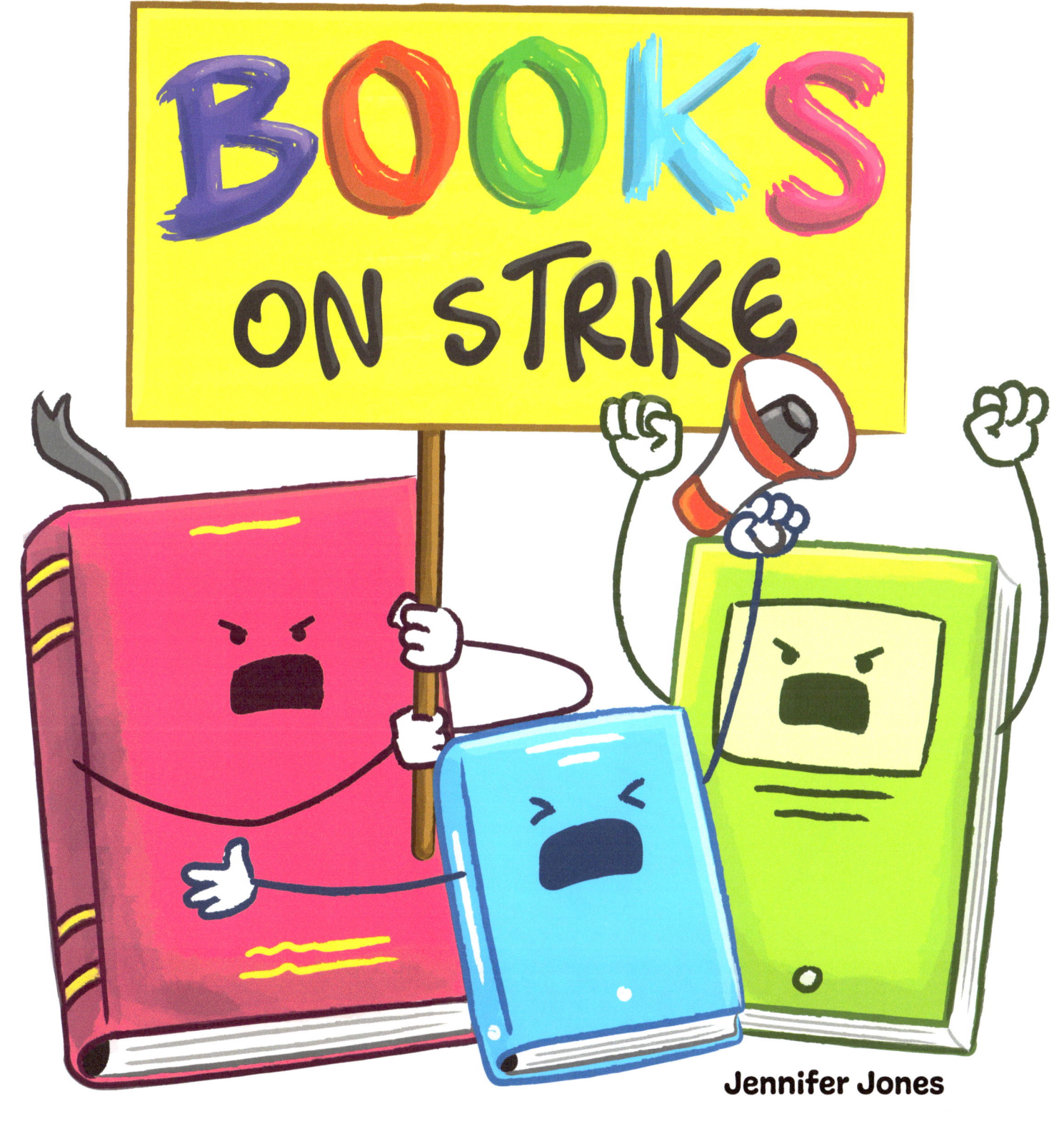

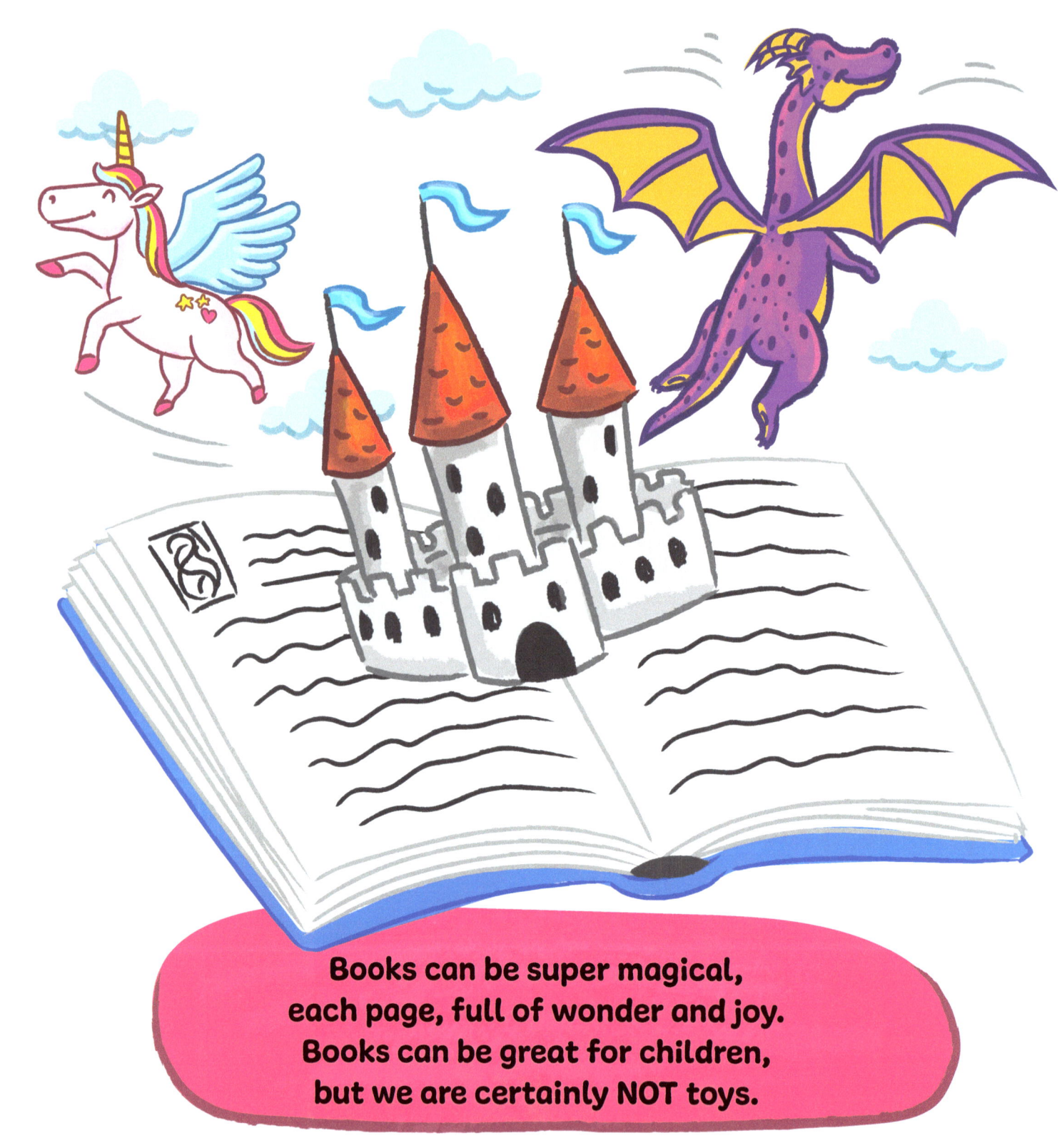

Books can be super magical,
each page, full of wonder and joy.
Books can be great for children,
but we are certainly NOT toys.

We're tossed and thrown around
and even held just by our spine.
We are put away without care,
tossed in the toy bin each time.

You lose us among other things,
never to be seen again.
You promise your teacher you'll take care of us,
but we'd like to ask you — WHEN?

It's not just where you place us.
It's how you treat our pages.
Sometimes the abuse isn't all at once.
Sometimes you hurt us in stages.

You lick our pages just for fun.

You chew us on our spines.

We've told each other "It will get better.

We just have to give it time."

Sometimes you rip us up
as if our words don't matter at all.
The adults say, "Books are important,"
but you make us feel so small.

We're not for you to sit on
or treat however you'd like.
You haven't treated us with respect,
so that's why we're on strike!

The children came back and wrote a letter in reply:

We promise to put you back on the shelves,

you know, the place that you belong.

We won't throw you in the toy bins.

We realize now that has been wrong.

And when someone is reading from you,
sharing the beautiful stories you have within,
we won't yell over the readers or not pay attention,
starting from the moment the reader begins.

We promise not to use you as a weapon to play and hit our friend.
It's not really good behavior.
We promise the book abuse will end!

www.ingramcontent.com/pod-product-compliance
Lightning Source LLC
Chambersburg PA
CBHW041522070526
44585CB00002B/47